I0016704

# Amazon Echo Dot:

## *The Ultimate 2017 User Guide & Manual*

Matthews M. Rothschild

The following eBook is reproduced below with the goal of providing information that is as accurate and reliable as possible. Regardless, purchasing this eBook can be seen as consent to the fact that both the publisher and the author of this book are in no way experts on the topics discussed within and that any recommendations or suggestions that are made herein are for entertainment purposes only. Professionals should be consulted as needed prior to undertaking any of the action endorsed herein.

This declaration is deemed fair and valid by both the American Bar Association and the Committee of Publishers Association and is legally binding throughout the United States.

Furthermore, the transmission, duplication or reproduction of any of the following work including specific information will be considered an illegal act irrespective of if it is done electronically or in print.

This extends to creating a secondary or tertiary copy of the work or a recorded copy and is only allowed with express written consent from the Publisher. All additional right reserved.

The information in the following pages is broadly considered to be a truthful and accurate account of facts and as such any inattention, use or misuse of the information in question by the reader will render any resulting actions solely under their purview. There are no scenarios in which the publisher or the original author of this work can be in any fashion deemed liable for any hardship or damages that may befall them after undertaking information described herein.

Additionally, the information in the following pages is intended only for informational purposes and should thus be thought of as universal. As befitting its nature, it is presented without assurance regarding its prolonged validity or interim quality. Trademarks that are mentioned are done without written consent and can in no way be considered an endorsement from the trademark holder.

# Table of Contents

# Introduction

Congratulations on downloading *Amazon Echo Dot: User Guide & Manual* and thank you for doing so. While for many people, their current level of technology accessibility means that they are inundated with it at every turn, there are still those out there who, for one reason or another, simply can't cross that technological hurdle. Voice recognition software then offers them access to an entire new world, one where they don't need to worry about dealing with an interface any more complicated than the human voice.

Just because you can control something with your voice, however, doesn't mean that you will automatically know which questions to ask which is why the following chapters will discuss everything you need to know in order to making using your new device as simple and painless as possible. First you will learn about the Echo Dot and which version of the device is best for you, including which generation of the device as well as the other products in the same wheelhouse. With an understanding of what you need, you will then learn all of the ins and outs of setting up the device to your exact specifications including getting Alexa used to your voice and setting her up just the way you like.

From there, you will learn how to personalize Alexa in countless different ways by teaching her specific skills related to practically everything you imagine. With a look at the broadest possibilities, you will then learn about many of the more practical, every day uses of the Echo Dot. With the basics out of the way there is then a deep dive into the possibilities that Alexa presents both in terms of entertainment and smart home options. Finally, you will learn about the Echo Dot's more extraneous features including Easter eggs sure to delight pop culture junkies of all stripes, creeds and fandoms.

There are plenty of books on this subject on the market, thanks again for choosing this one! Every effort was made to ensure it is full of as much useful information as possible, please enjoy!

# Chapter 1: What is Echo Dot?

The Amazon Echo Dot at first glance may look unimpressive and small; however, it is anything but ordinary. It's an instantaneous, hands-free, voice-operated computer that takes up about as much space a hockey puck. It's computational power is used, mostly, for waiting. Waiting for what you ask? The seven far-reaching microphones are always on, always listening, and always waiting for the go word: "Alexa" (or several other options if you prefer).

The Alexa Voice Service is the brain and heart of the Amazon Echo Dot. The Alexa Voice Service is located in the cloud, meaning it can access the combined knowledge of the internet, as well as all of your personal data (that it's allowed, of course) and then respond instantly and accurately to hundreds of different questions and commands. As such, this means Alexa can tell you a personalized newsreel, convert millimeters to inches or order you your favorite pizza, all with just the touch of a button. You can also do things such as listen to your favorite book via Audible or get lost into a Choose Your Own Adventure story. The possibilities are endless with the Amazon Echo Dot and the Alexa Voice Service, which is always learning, always getting smarter.

The Amazon Echo Dot is a marvel in many ways, and when compared to sister and brother devices as well as it's competition it truly does stand out as an amazing smart home device.

## Echo vs. Echo Dot

There is one glaringly obvious difference between Amazon's Echo and Echo Dot: the size. The Amazon Echo is a whopping 7.8 inches taller than the Echo Dot (for a total of a 9.25 inch device). This is due to the incredibly immersive, 360-degree audio speaker that features a two and a half inch sub woofer and a two-inch tweeter. While the speaker is of great quality, Amazon's first Echo device comes at the highest price of the three devices: $179.99 in comparison to $129.99 for the Amazon Echo Tap and $49.99 for the Echo Dot.

Ultimately, the Echo Dot can do everything that the regular Echo can achieve—the only thing lost in size was the speaker. Both devices are always listening, and are completely hands-free. The Echo Dot can also be connected to your house speakers, unlike the Echo, via Bluetooth or a 3.5mm audio cable (not included). Thus, if you already have a speaker system in your home that you enjoy, the Echo Dot becomes the smarter choice due to cost effectiveness and versatility.

**Echo vs. Echo Tap**

The Echo Tap is a very middle-of-the-ground Alexa-device. It's the median priced device, and medium sized (an inch taller than the Echo Dot and about a pound total in weight) device in the line up for sure, but there are some differing features in the Tap. For one, it's portable. All other Echo devices require being plugged into the wall, but the Amazon Echo Tap can give up to nine hours of audio playback on a single charge. It has a more quality speaker than the Echo Dot does, and guarantees a great, crisp sound on the go.

Another huge difference with the Echo Tap is that it is not always listening; therefor you cannot wake it with a voice command by the others. To wake the Tap device, you have to make physical contact with it, which can be a downfall in some occurrences.

Where the Tap adds portability, it loses in some functionality. It is still a great device if it suits your needs, but for the price the Echo Dot still offers more overall.

**Gen 1 vs. Gen 2**

Not many people are aware that a first generation Echo Dot even existed, because it was not originally sold on Amazon's website to all customers—only to those who already had an Alexa-enabled device (an Echo, Tap, Fire TV, or already in their homes. The changes are minimal, and were made to improve functionality and affordability.

The changes in look are subtle, but are there if you're looking. For instance, the second generation Echo Dot features a sleeker finish, and is just barely smaller (and lighter) than its predecessor. Looking even closer, its speaker grill design is slightly altered. Furthermore, the sheeny White Pearl color wasn't available until the second generation.

The first generation Amazon Echo Dot was also a bit steeper in price, keeping it from being the "every room" type of device Amazon was aiming for. It sold for $89.99, while new Echo Dot goes for $49.99 brand new. Some cost effective changes made to the first gen Dot were doing away with the rotating volume wheel and replacing it with volume up and down buttons, as well as not including a 3.5mm audio cable in the packaging (for connecting to speakers).

There were some huge software updates between generations. Before if you had multiple Echo devices in your home you would be greeted with a chorus of responses; that is no longer the case with Echo Spatial Perception that comes built into the second generation Echo Dot. Echo Spatial Perception (ESP) enables Alexa to respond smartly from whichever device picks up the command with the most clarity. This feature was given in an update to the previous generational Amazon Echo devices, and will actually only increase in intelligence as time goes on. The second generation Amazon also features a new speech processor that is better at picking up commands.

In general, all changes made between generations were received well and really acknowledged some of the customers' grievances with the first generation device.

**Benefits of Echo Dot Over Other Tech**

Following the success of the first Amazon Echo, competition was bound to be in the works. And so it was.

Google has responded with its own smart speaker voice-controlled device, the Google Home. The Google Home works similar to the Amazon Echo and Echo Dot, with the "always listening" technology and using its incredibly large backer of information to help users in any way they can. It features a nice stereo that can fully surround any room just like the Echo, but has a hard time connecting to existing home stereo systems. And for the price ($129.99), if you already have the home speaker, Amazon's Echo Dot gives you so much more functionality, customization and full home integration for the price.

Overall, the price and incredible functionality of the Amazon Echo Dot makes it an incredible addition to any smart home, or even the start of one. As long as you have the proper speaker equipment to which connect your Echo Dot, it truly is the best fifty bucks you may ever spend.

# Chapter 2: Setting Up Your Echo Dot

The Amazon Echo Dot comes in pretty blue little box, with only four things needed to get you started:

1. Quick Start Guide—this will provide useful information regarding the initial set up if you are a first time user of an Amazon Echo device
2. 9-Watt Power Adapter—a more powerful adapter than most cell phone charger adapter, and how you plug the device into the wall
3. Micro-USB Cable—for connect the device to the power adapter
4. Device—sleek, covered in protective tapes, and fits in the palm of your hand

Upon inspection, you will see that there are four buttons and a light ring atop the device:

15

1. Microphone Off Button—disables Echo Dot device from always listening, you'll have to press the button again to get the device to respond (the light ring will be red if you turn off microphones)

2. Action Button—alternative method for waking your device, can be used to turns of alarms/timers, also launches Wi-Fi Setup Mode after being pressed for five seconds

3. Volume Buttons—straightforward volume up and down buttons, and while you're adjusting the volume the light right will display your volume level in white (volume is also numerically represented as one through ten for Alexa)

4. Light Ring—how Alexa can visually communicate its status condition to users:

   • Blue with rotating cyan lights = device turning on

- Blue with cyan pointing at speaker = Alexa is processing command
- Lights completely off = device is in always-listening mode, and ready to respond to a request (assuming the device is plugged in)
- Orange spinning light = device is working to connect to Wi-Fi network
- Violet light continuously oscillating = time to troubleshoot Wi-Fi connection

Finally, there are two jacks on the side of the device, one for the power cord and one for an audio cord if you decided to forgo Bluetooth connectivity.

Before you go much further on getting your Echo Dot device set up, go to the app store on your cellular device and download the companion Alexa App. This application is free to download from current app stores, and is an extra useful accessory to your user experience with Alexa. Note that you can also get the full Alexa application functionality off of a computer that is connected to the Internet (and has downloaded most updated version of Internet Explorer, Microsoft Edge, Safari, and Chrome). An amazon account is necessary to move forward and free, so if you are without you will need to follow that process as well.

With the app downloaded, plug your device into the wall. The light ring on top of the device will instantly turn blue once plugged in, and then the color will switch to orange as Alexa wakes on your brand new Echo Dot for the very first time. From here, use the Alexa App to get your device connected to Wi-Fi, and viola, your device is completely set up and the possibilities are endless.

Note: This is also a great time to get your initial Bluetooth set up with your preferred speaker/sound system. After you initially connect the devices, you can say "Alexa, Bluetooth" to connect quickly with paired devices (speaker must be on or connected to smart outlet that turns with predetermined command).

## Waking Alexa

The Echo Dot is always listening, but it is really only listening for a specific word, called the "wake word". The default wake word on the Echo Dot is "Alexa", for example if you were looking to hear the weather you'd say, "Alexa, give me the weather forecast for this weekend".

If you have an Alexa living in the house or just want to switch the wake word for any reason, you can change it to either "Echo", "Amazon", or "Computer" (one of many throw outs on the Echo device for fandoms, specifically Star Trek in this instance). To do this, use the navigational panel in the Alexa App (three horizontal lines) and click Settings. Click on your Echo Dot device (or whichever device you want to change the wake word on) and you'll find Wake Word at the bottom of the screen. Save, and you're wake word is changed!

## Using Multiple Accounts

It is possible to more than one Amazon accounts your Echo Dot device. In Settings in the Alexa app, scroll near the bottom again and select Household Profile, and then follow the easy on-screen instructions and enter the necessary information to add a new user. Finish by clicking the Join Household button, and then you are able to share music libraries, books, and lists among users!

If you wish to switch accounts, say "Alexa, switch to Tom's profile " or "Switch accounts" if you only have two accounts on the device. Check the active profile by asking, "Alexa, which profile am I using?"

Just to note, there aren't currently and parental control systems necessarily in place for the Alexa Voice Service, but Alexa does play it safe and deflects curious questions that should be directed to parents. Parents should review any content that enabled on the Echo Dot, as it third party and loosely monitored for child appropriateness.

Also, the Echo Dot keeps a recording of every command every spoken. This is in the fine print and not necessarily uncommon or illegal, but some may opt to not have a log of every thing they've ever asked Alexa. Now, this information is collected for the purpose of research and development—this is how your device learns about your vocal profile. If you wish to proceed, you can go to the Manage Your Devices/Content page on Amazon (www.amazon.com/myx) and find Your Devices>{Your Echo Dot}. From here, find Manage Voice Recordings and click delete (you will get a warning message about the Alexa Voice Service not running as accurately, but it's unlikely you'll notice too big of a difference).

# Chapter 3: Alexa's Got Skills

Skills are the building block for customizing your Amazon Echo Dot experience, and how you are able to get the most out of your device. Enabling these Skills allow Alexa to accomplish a variety of things: with Skills, Alexa can give you a ten minute recipe, tell you about possible flight delays, or lead you on a guided meditation. Skills are what make Alexa even better, and more and more Skills are always becoming available to enable on your device!

Think of skills as you would applications downloaded on a cell phone. They have to first be enabled for you to use them, and one real beauty of it is that you're not bogging your device down—this information is kept in the cloud, meaning your Echo Dot device is only going to get better, faster, and smarter! There are three easy ways to enable Skills:

1. In the Alexa app, drop down the left navigation menu and find Skills. Here you can search or browse by category

2. You enable skills directly using your voice, say "Alexa, enable the Bacon Facts Skill." Sometimes this can take just a moment for her to learn the skill.

3. There's also a web page for Alexa Skills on Amazon's website, with similar function and design as the Alexa app.

Take some time to explore all of the Alexa Skills out there. The voice platform is an all-new way for businesses to reach customers, and companies are rising to the occasion. And there are plenty of skills out there for pure enjoyment as well.

## Basic Alexa Skills

There are some Skills that come ready-to-go on your new Amazon Echo Dot. These skills are dead useful in your every day life, so it's worth learning how to use them to their full potential.

## Setting Alarms and Timers

If your Echo Dot is a bedside companion, you can have Alexa set your alarms for you with simple voice commands! Just say, "Alexa, set an alarm for 9:00 am." Alexa can also set a repeating alarm if you ask her to. Go to the Alexa app for further alarm customizations, such as alarm tone. And don't worry—as long as your device is plugged in the alarm will sound no matter what.

Setting a timer is a similar process. Say, "Alexa, set a timer for an hour and five minutes," and you're set! Use this handy skill to help you out in the kitchen or if you need to help enforce 25-5 productive rule (25 minutes productive, 5 minute break).

## Using Google Calendar & Lists

In addition to waking you up and keeping you timely, your Amazon Echo Dot can help you keep track of important dates and events! First, you will have to link a Google Calendar Account in the Alexa app. If you don't already have a free Google account for your calendar, go to _https://calendar.google.com_ and follow the on-screen set up. Use the left navigational panel to navigate to Settings, and then Google Calendar>Link to put in your account information. Use the following format of commands to operate the calendar feature on your Echo Dot:

- "Alexa, what's on my calendar next Tuesday?"
- "Add 'Dinner with Parents' to my calendar for next Friday at seven o'clock p.m."
- "Alexa, when is my next event?"
- For Alexa to guide you through adding an event say, "Add an event to my calendar."

Another great organizational tool the Echo Dot provides is its list capabilities. Alexa can keep track of both your shopping list and to-do list, and repeat them back to you whenever you need. You can even set it up so that Alexa sends your Shopping List to you via e-mail when it's time to go shopping!

- To add an item to your shopping list: "Alexa, add Batteries to my Shopping List."
- To add something to your to do list: "Alexa, add Vacuum Living Room to my To-Do List."
- To review your lists: "Alexa, what's on my Shopping/To-Do List?"

You can also review, manage, and print your lists in the Alexa app or on your computer, as well as see a compilation of your finished tasks! Lists will also be shared across common users, meaning anyone can ask at any time and get the full lists.

*Getting Your Customized News*

Alexa is able to stream you a live feed of news that's important to you from handpicked sources, called a Flash Briefing. To get started setting up your very own Flash Briefing, first head over to the Alexa

App. There are two ways you can add/remove media outlets from your Flash Breifing.

1. Drop the left navigational panel down, and find Settings>Flash Briefing. Once here, you are able to completely customize the headlines, weather updates, and shows that you want to hear during your Briefing. You are also able to arrange the content so it is given to you in any order you would like.

2. Use the left navigational panel to access Alexa Skills. There is a Flash Briefing category, and you would enable these like you would any other skills.

To start hearing your news, ask Alexa, "What's new?" or "What's my Flash Briefing?" You can move quickly through stories by saying, "Next", or "Previous", or "Cancel" to close Flash Briefing.

Note that if you have multiple accounts on your Echo Dot device, you may want to check that you are for certain the active account as Flash Briefings to stay custom per account.

*Shopping On Your Device*

You are able to order Prime-eligible Amazon merchandise via your Echo Dot! Take note, it is important that you set up purchasing via Voice prior to anything else. There are a few requirements to enable Voice Purchasing on your device: a 1-click enabled payment method (tied to a U.S. bank), a U.S. shipping address, and of course an Amazon Prime account. For added security, it is recommended that you set up a four-digit confirmation pin that would be required to make purchases from your device. You can do this in the Alexa app under Manage Voice Purchase Settings.

To shop with Alexa, utilize these commands:

- "Order an Echo Dot."—Used to order any single Prime-eligible item (up to 12 in quantity)

- "Add an Echo Dot to Cart"—To continue shopping and place total order at once, "Finish order," to finalize purchases
- "Reorder toilet paper."—Can be used to reorder any item previously ordered from your device
- "Where's my stuff?"—Keep track of your purchase status/delivery, can alternatively say, "Alexa, track my order."
- "Cancel my order."—If you made a mistake ordering or wish to cancel your order right away for whatever reason

Doing your Amazon shopping is not only fun, but it really helps save you on time!

**List of currently active Alexa skills**

*1-2-3 Math*

**Access by saying:** [Command word], Open 1,2,3

Tests your elementary mathematics topics like after, before, between; greater or lesser, more or less, addition, subtraction etc.

*1-Minute Mindfulness*

**Access by saying:** [Command word], let me have a minute of meditation

Provides 60 seconds of peaceful sound to aid in meditation.

*21 Dayz*

**Access by saying:** [Command word], begin 21 Dayz

This skill will allow you to let Alexa help you to keep up with a skill for the 21 days you need in order to ensure it becomes a habit.

*4AFart*

**Access by saying:** [Command word], Ask For A Fart

Let Alexa be your virtual whoopee cushion.

*7-Minute Workout*

**Access by saying:** [Command word], Start 7-minute workout

Quick workout designed to lower stress and get the blood flowing

## *7Sigma*

**Access by saying:** [Command word], ask 7 Sigma for my update

Check on all the disparate elements of your current 7 sigma project including data from numerous different sources

## *Abra*

**Access by saying:** [Command word], start Abra

This is a 20 questions game where you think of a famous person, living or dead, real or imagined and Alexa will be able to figure out who it is.

## *AccuWeather*

**Access by saying:** [Command word], start AccuWeather

Stay connected to the latest in weather forecasting with AccuWeather – Weather for Life. Ask for weather alerts, sunrise, sunset, moonset, moonrise & moon phases

*Acoustic Metronome*

**Access by saying:** [Command word], open metronome

Having trouble keeping the beat? TsaTsaTzu can help you keep your groove with a nice acoustical drum beat to help you keep time.


*Admirer*

**Access by saying:** [Command word], tell my admirer to make me smile

Have Alexa pay you a compliment


*Adventure*

**Access by saying:** [Command word], play Dave of Doom

Provides a Choose Your Own Adventure like


*Age Calculator*

**Access by saying:** [Command word], ask Age Calculator the age of a person on [specific date]

This skill can provide you with the age of any person in days, months and years.

*Word Master Game*

**Access by saying:** [Command word], Word Master

Challenge yourself to expand your vocabulary and beat your high score in the process.


*Angry Bard*

**Access by saying:** [Command word], ask Angry Bard for a burn

This skill will throw out a Shakespearean insult at any time.


*AnyMote Smart Remote*

**Access by saying:** [Command word], ask AnyMote

Use your voice to control your smart television


*AOL*

**Access by saying:** [Command word], ask AOL for headlines

Up to the minute entertainment, finance, sports and political news.

## Animal Game

**Access by saying:** [Command word], start Animal Game

If you think of an animal, real or imaginary, Alexa will ask you questions in order to determine what it is.

## Animal Sounds

**Access by saying:** [Command word], ask Animal Sounds the noise an [animal] makes.

This skill will allow Alexa to reply with a wide variety of different animal noises.

## Area Code

**Access by saying:** [Command word], ask where is [area code] is

Alexa will tell you the physical location of any area code

## Ask Earthquakes

**Access by saying:** [Command word], What's shakin'

This skill will provide recent relevant earthquake information

## *Ask My Buddy*

**Access by saying:** [Command word], ask My Buddy to help me get started

This skill will help you to easily send a text message, email or voice message to one or more of your contacts

## *AskAboutTrump*

**Access by saying:** [Command word], ask Trump [simple question]

This skill will allow Alexa to answer simple questions as if she were the President Trump.

**Access by saying:** [Command word], *ask Audio Goal for a goal*

Celebrate any success in the most appropriate way possible.

## *Baby Names*

**Access by saying:** [Command word], tell me about [baby name]

Find out the popularity of any name dating back all the way to the 1880s.

## Baseball Archive

**Access by saying:** [Command word], ask Baseball Archive about [player name]

Get information and statistics for any player in the history of Major League Baseball.

## Basket Savings

**Access by saying:** [Command word], Ask Basket Savings if [item is on sale near location]

Find prices on a wide variety of common grocery items.

## Beat Cylinder

**Access by saying:** [Command word], launch Beat Cylinder

This skill will teach Alexa to beat box in a variety of different styles.

## Beat the Dealer

**Access by saying:** [Command word], ask the dealer to deal the cards

Beat the dealer in this game of Blackjack.

*Beer Trivia*

**Access by saying:** [Command word], launch Beer Trivia

This skill launches an in-depth beer trivia game.

*Best Picture*

**Access by saying:** [Command word], start Best Picture Oscars

This skill will allow Alexa to tell you who won the Oscar for best picture for the past 30 years

*Bible App*

**Access by saying:** [Command word] read [Bible verse]

This skill will allow Alexa to read out any of the verses in the King James Bible.

*Bingo*

**Access by saying:** [Command word], open Bingo

This skill allows Alexa to call a bingo game.

*Bubble Boy*

**Access by saying:** [Command word], ask Bubble Boy to tell me a joke

This skill allows Alexa to repeat numerous quotes from the once popular television show *Seinfeld*.

*Calculator*

**Access by saying:** [Command word] ask calculator to [do math problem]

This skill turns Alexa into a voice controlled calculator.

*Capital Quiz*

**Access by saying:** [Command word], tell Capital Quiz to start practicing

This skill allows Alexa to quiz you on you all the US state capitals.

*Cat Facts*

**Access by saying:** [Command word], open Cat Facts

This skill allows Alexa to learn everything you ever wanted to know about cats and also to have a burning desire to share.

## Christmas Caroler

**Access by saying:** [Command word], spread holiday cheer

This skill teaches Alexa numerous classic Christmas songs.

## Code Phrase

**Access by saying:** [Command word], ask for a code phrase

This skill teaches Alexa how to provide code words for all of your most secret projects.

## Combat

**Access by saying:** [Command word], open Combat and [name target to use item to attack]

This skill allows Alexa to simulate numerous different combat scenarios.

## Conversation Starter

**Access by saying:** [Command word], open Conversation Starter

This skill provides Alexa the ability to provide you will all the best conversation starters.

*Cookbook*

**Access by saying:** [Command word], ask cookbook how to [prepare simple recipe]

This skill turns Alexa into an expert chef who can provide you with all sort of meal based information


*Covisint Trivia*

**Access by saying:** [Command word], launch Cove Trivia

This skill will provide Alexa with everything she needs to quiz you on the  Covisint company.


*Cricket Quiz*

**Access by saying:** [Command word], launch cricket quiz

This skill provides Alexa with everything she needs to quiz you on the current state of the fine game of cricket.


*CryptoCurrency*

**Access by saying:** [Command word], ask my crypto what is the price of bitcoin?

This skill will allow Alexa to quote the current price of bitcoins at any time.

## Crystal Ball

**Access by saying:** [Command word], launch Crystal Ball

This skill will provide Alexa with the ability to answer any yes or no question.

## Currency Converter

**Access by saying:** [Command word], ask Currency Converter to convert [an amount of one currency to another]

This skill will allow Alexa to convert one currency to another.

## Daily Word

**Access by saying:** [Command word], open Daily Word

This skill will teach Alexa a new word every single day of the year.

## Dice Bag

**Access by saying:** [Command word], tell Dice Bag to roll for me

This skill will provide Alexa with the ability to roll dice of all shapes and sizes.

*Dino Trivia*

**Access by saying:** [Command word], Open dino trivia

This skill will teach Alexa everything you ever wanted to know about dinosaurs and also gives her the ability to quiz you based on what she knows.

*Dog Facts*

**Access by saying:** [Command word], tell me a dog fact

This skill will teach Alexa everything you ever wanted to know about dogs so she can tell you fresh facts whenever you ask.

*Domain Name Info*

**Access by saying:** [Command word] launch domain name info for [domain name]

This skill will allow Alexa to access numerous details about a given domain name, all you need to do is ask.

*Domino's*

**Access by saying:** [Command word], place my Domino's Easy Order

This skill will allow you to program in a standard order to the nearest Domino's location

*Drive Time*

**Access by saying:** [Command word], launch Drive Time

This skill will allow Alexa to provide you with the estimated drive time between two locations.

*Drop Some Knowledge*

**Access by saying:** [Command word], ask drop some knowledge to tell me about [anything or anyone]

This skill provides Alexa with a direct link to the Google Knowledge Graph API which means it can tell you about anything or anyone.

*Eliza*

**Access by saying:** [Command word], start Eliza

This skill turns Alexa into your own person therapist.


*ELLE Horoscopes*

**Access by saying:** [Command word], what is the horoscope for [zodiac sign]

Open Alexa to the wonders of the zodiac and hear your horoscope every day.


*Email Assistant*

**Access by saying:** [Command word], open Email Assistant

This skill connects Alexa directly to your favorite email client.


*Essential Trivia*

**Access by saying:** [Command word], open Essential Trivia

This skill provides Alexa with access to a wide variety of trivia facts that absolutely everyone needs to know.

## Event Guide

**Access by saying:** [Command word], ask Event Guide what's going on today in [city name]

Turn Alexa into the most connected person you know and she will always be able to point you towards the most far out happening around.

## Famous Quotes

**Access by saying:** [Command word], tell me a quote

This skill teaches Alexa a wide variety of famous quotations from both pop culture and literature.

## Fantasy Football

**Access by saying:** [Command word], ask Fantasy Football Nerd [team] news

This skill ensures that Alexa is really, really into fantasy football.

## Five Card Draw

**Access by saying:** [Command word] start five card draw

This skill allows Alexa to automatically deal out a hand of 5 card draw

*FlightSearch*

**Access by saying:** [Command word], Ask Flight Search for [flight information]

This skill will search out the five cheapest flights for the details you enter and have Alexa read them aloud.

*Focus Word*

Alexa, open Focus Word

Focus Word provides an inspirational word and statement about the word to serve as a point of focus for meditation or for the day.

*Football Trivia*

Alexa, open Football Trivia

Trivia game asking questions that pertain to professional American Football.

*Fortune Cookie*

Alexa, open Fortune Cookie

Get a fortune cookie, read to you and receive your own Mega Millions or Powerball numbers.

## Founding Father Quotes

Alexa, ask founding fathers for a quote
Get quotes from our Founding Fathers, the political philosophers who inspired them, and their modern successors.

## Glympse

**Access by saying:** [Command word], ask Glympse where is [family member or friend]?
This skill lets various individuals track one another's location via Alexa

## Gold Bug

**Access by saying:** [Command word], ask Gold Bug what's the price of [gold/silver/oil]
This skill provides Alexa with the ability to access the up to the minute prices of oil, silver and gold.

## Guess The Number

**Access by saying:** [Command word], launch Guess the Number

This skill will teach Alexa to pick a number between 1 and 100 and encourage you to guess it.

*Guitar Tuner*

**Access by saying:** [Command word], ask Guitar Tuner to tune my guitar

This skill turn Alexa into an audio guitar tuner

*Hacker News*

**Access by saying:** [Command word] open Hacker News

This skill allows Alexa to jack into cyberspace and interface with all of the latest hacker headlines.

*Haiku*

**Access by saying:** [Command word], ask Haiku for a poem

This skill will allow

Alexa to generate

Randomized haikus

*Happy Birthday*

**Access by saying:** [Command word], launch Happy Birthday

This skill teaches Alexa the Happy Birthday song and causes her to sing it on command

### HomeSeer Home Automation Skill

**Access by saying:** [Command word], tell HomeSeer to [operate device]

This skill allows Alexa to directly interface with the HomeSeer home automation system

### House Band

**Access by saying:** [Command word], launch House Band

This skill allows Alexa to access a JRiver Media Center music server including the ability to create new playlists, listen to saved tracks and more.

### HuffPost

**Access by saying:** [Command word], ask HuffPost for headlines

This skill allows Alexa to read the current crop of *Huffington Post* headlines

### Impossibly Hard Major League Baseball Quiz

**Access by saying:** [Command word], launch Impossible Baseball Quiz

This will provide Alexa with access to the hardest quiz about the great sport of baseball ever devised.

*IndianFacts*

**Access by saying:** [Command word], tell me an Indian fact

This skill will provide Alexa with access to a little known fact about the country of India.

*Innkeeper Emotes for Hearthstone*

**Access by saying:** [Command word], ask the innkeeper to say hello to the mage

This skill connects Alexa directly to your current game of Hearthstone.

*InsultiBot*

**Access by saying:** [Command word], open InsultiBot

This skill gives Alexa access to a bit of a mean streak, it may be what she really thinks of you.

*JavaScript Quiz*

**Access by saying:** [Command word], Launch JavaScript Quiz

This skill makes Alexa a whiz at the programing language JavaScript, so much so that she can even quiz you on the details that you need to know.

*Jazz Trivia*

**Access by saying:** [Command word], start Jazz Trivia

This skill will allow Alexa to either test your general knowledge of Jazz trivia or to enlighten you on facts that you didn't know or would never have guessed.

*Jeopardy!*

**Access by saying:** [Command word], Play Jeopardy

This skill adds a number of new questions to the Jeporday game that comes preinstalled on the Echo Dot.

*Jokes++*

**Access by saying:** [Command word], ask Jokes Plus Plus for a joke

This skill allows Alexa to get back to her roots by giving her access to countless different jokes based around the computer sciences.

*Knock Knock Jokes*

**Access by saying:** [Command word], ask knock knock

This skill teaches Alexa a wide variety of knock, knock jokes sure to please children of all ages.

*Laugh Box*

**Access by saying:** [Command word], open laugh box

If you are in need of a sympathetic audience, look no further than this skill which allows Alexa to laugh in several different ways.

*Let's Multiply*

**Access by saying:** [Command word], open let's multiply

This skill will allow Alexa to tutor anyone interested in improving their knowledge of the multiplication tables all the way from 1x1 to 12x12.

## *LIFX*

**Access by saying:** [Command word], tell LIFX to [activate specific lights]

This skill allows Alexa to tap into any outlet that has been connected to a LIFX system and activate it automatically.

## *Long Weekend Info*

**Access by saying:** [Command word], open Long Weekend

This skill teaches Alexa one thing and one thing only, when the next 3-day weekend is and the number of days until it gets here.

## *Lotto Now*

**Access by saying:** [Command word], ask Lotto Now for Powerball numbers

This skill will allow Alexa to generate a random string of Powerball numbers. You can't win if you don't play.

## Lyrical

**Access by saying:** [Command word], open Lyrical

This skill turns Alexa into a musical genius, she will be able to tell you the name of almost any song as long as you can provide the lyrics.

## Magic 8-Ball

**Access by saying:** [Command word], ask Magic 8-Ball [an appropriate question]

This skill turns Alexa into your very out audio Magic 8-ball.

## Market News

**Access by saying:** [Command word], ask Market for news

This skill turns Alexa into a fiend for financial news allowing her to tap into CNBC, Reuters, Wall Street Journal, Mark Watch and more.

*Math Mania*

**Access by saying:** [Command word], play Math Mania

Gives Alexa access to a simple math game

*Math Puzzles*

**Access by saying:** [Command word], open Math Puzzles

This gives Alexa access to a game where she will provide sequences of numbers for you to fill in the missing numbers in the sequence.

*Memory Master*

**Access by saying:** [Command word], open Memory Master

This skill gives Alexa access to the classic game of Memory Master

*Meteor Showers*

**Access by saying:** [Command word], Ask meteor showers what is happening tonight

This skill will teach Alexa all about the celestial events that are happening in your area and where to go to get the best view.

## Mirror, Mirror

**Access by saying:** [Command word], Open Mirror, Mirror

This skill will make Alexa very good at giving compliments and ready to provide you with a confidence boost at a moment's notice.

## MotoQuote

**Access by saying:** [Command word] ask MotoQuote for a Quote

This skill provides Alexa access to a database of new positive quotes every single day.

## Movie Info

**Access by saying:** [Command word], ask movie info about [movie title]

This skill turns Alexa into a cinephile, she will be able to tell you all of the relevant details about any movie based solely on its title.

### Mr Junky Food

**Access by saying:** [Command word], ask Mr. Junky Food what to eat today

For junk food fans, this skill will allow Alexa to teach you about a wide variety of snack options that go well above and beyond the standard.

### My Dermatologist

**Access by saying:** [Command word], ask My Dermatologist [skincare question]

This skill will turn Alexa into your own personal dermatologist capable of answering a host of important skincare questions.

### Mystery Castle

**Access by saying:** [Command word], launch Mystery Castle

Explore an audio adventure where you and Alexa move through a castle, collecting treasure and avoiding traps.

## Nikola Tesla Trivia

**Access by saying:** [Command word], ask Nikola Tesla

This skill brings Alexa in line with modern internet culture and its love of all things Nikola Tesla with plenty of fascinating facts about a great inventor.

## Northern Lights Forecast

**Access by saying:** [Command word], ask Aurora

This skill will provide Alexa with a direct link to details about the current state of the Northern Lights.

# Chapter 4: Using Your Echo Dot Everyday

Once you start enabling new Skills for Alexa to use, her abilities to assist you in your everyday life may astound you! Besides making lists and keeping your calendar straight, Alexa can also any trivial question you throw her way (via her deep knowledge bank from Wikipedia), be the perfect sous chef, or even provide you with some inspiration when needed!

## Alexa In The Kitchen

There are many great places to station your Echo Dot, and the kitchen is one of them. This is because of the vast amount of culinary skills available (and that number is always increasing) to make Alexa the perfect cooking companion! Use the timer in the kitchen to help keep track of time, ask for a quick measuring conversion if you need one—just say, "Alexa, how many teaspoons are in a tablespoon?" You can also get basic nutritional information on common foods by asking Alexa, "How many carbohydrates/calories are in a banana?"

No matter what your skill level is in the kitchen, there is guaranteed an Alexa Skill out there to improve your cooking experience! Here are some useful Skills to enable for Alexa:

- Having a mental block of what to cook for dinner? There are a plethora of recipe Skills available on the Alexa app. Check out Hellman's, Campbell's, Allrecipes, Recipe Buddy, Food Network, and more! There are also recipe Skills that can give you a recipe based off of what you actually have in the fridge.

- Speaking of your fridge, you can keep a running inventory of what's in your fridge (and get reminders when something is about to expire) with the My Chef – Kitchen Assistant. This skill can even add the expired items to your Shopping List!

- If your cooking equipment game is on the techy side, enable the Joule skill to control the temperature on the Joule Sous Vide.

- If you are looking for beverage recipes, Alexa has that covered as well. Enable the Bartender or the Mixologist Skills and ask for the recipe to a classic Tom Collins or Manhattan. Enable the Patron Skill to find a spicy margarita. There is also a Smoothies Skill for those with a blender an affinity for delicious smoothies!

- Some days you want to leave the cooking to others, and that's understandable. There are many local Skills available that allow you to voice-order delivery food. Dominoes and Wing Stop are just a few examples of restaurants jumping at the opportunity to be even more easily accessed by their customers than ever before!

- Or perhaps you'd like to find a new place to go to eat. Ask Alexa, "What's a Chinese restaurant close to me?" You can also use enable restaurant finder Skills if you're not quite finding what you want right away.

## More Practical Uses of Alexa

Alexa has more practicalities beyond being a kitchen assistant, though. She can make lightning quick mathematical equations and help you keep track of your finances as credit card companies and banks make their information accessible via this platform. For instance, if you were to enable the Capital One Skill and link your account information you could ask Alexa to, "Ask Capital One, what's my account summary?"

Another useful Skill to enable on Alexa: car service! Alexa can get you a ride with Lyft or Uber, all you need to do is just say the magic words, "Alexa, get me a ride." Also, there's no reason to be late for traffic anymore—if you have a specific destination set out, Alexa can tell you about the most recent update of a live traffic feed!

*Alexa Takes Care of Your Mind & Body*
Check out some of these Alexa Skills that are designed to improve your headspace and your physique!

- If you would like to workout but are low on time, the 7-Minute Workout Skill is your new best workout buddy! Enable and launch a quick workout that is guaranteed to get your heart pumping and calories burning! Or link your Fitbit to your Echo Dot, and ask Alexa how you're doing on steps for the day. Check out the Fitness category in the Alexa Skills page for more ways Alexa can help you get in shape.

- Feeling a tad bit uninspired? If you want to hear from some of the best speakers of our time, enable the Inspire Me Skill and have Alexa "inspire you". It definitely helps to hear from the greats!

- There's a full category for Zen and relaxation Skills on the Alexa app. These can guide you through a meditation lasting from a minute to an hour! There are even guided breathing exercises for when life does get a little stressful or overwhelming.

- Fall asleep to soothing ocean sounds or white noise if you have Alexa in your bedroom! Some of these Skills have even more cool effects, like growing quieter over a set period of time as you drift into a peaceful sleep.

- Tough life choice? Ask Alexa to "Flip a coin," or if things are really serious, ask the Magic 8 Ball.

New ways for your Amazon Echo Dot to make your life easier are constantly being developed! Check your Alexa App and the Things To Try section regularly to find even more ways to integrate Alexa into your everyday life!

# Chapter 5: Be Entertained By Your Echo Dot

Alexa makes life easier, sure, but she also makes life a bunch more fun! With your Echo Dot, you can stream all your favorite music, listen to your favorite books, and play for hours on the many Skills out there designed for pure entertainment purposes.

**Playing Your Music**

With your Amazon Echo Dot, you can access millions of songs on the Internet with just the power of your voice. As previously mentioned, the only downfall of the Echo Dot in comparison to the other Echo devices is that its speaker definitely leaves something to be desired. The Echo Dot does let you listen to music at a comfortable volume without speakers connected, but if you want any sound quality (or just louder sound in general), you will certainly want to connect a set of speakers to your device. You can also connect headphones to your device if so desired.

Presently, your Echo Dot can play music via Amazon Music, Spotify, TuneIn, Pandora, and iHeart Radio. The default music player is Amazon Music, so unless you specify differently in your command to Alexa, any music requests will be played through Amazon Music. Since Amazon Music is the home team music provider for the Echo Dot, there are some unique commands available through Amazon Music and the general commands for music are otherwise pretty straightforward:

- Not sure what to listen to? You can get started listening just by saying, "Alexa, play music." When you do this, Alexa will pick a station she thinks you might like! From here, use basic commands as needed: "next/skip", "pause", "loop", "repeat", and "stop".

- You can play a specific song by providing the title and artist (sometimes just the title will do). Alexa will first look for it on the default music player, so if Amazon Music is your default player and you want to play something from Spotify, be sure to specify. You can change the default music player in the Alexa app if you wish to (and then you wouldn't need to indicate the player anymore).

- It's worth getting an account to TuneIn or iHeart Radio account to listen to public radio. Try playing a local radio station! Just say, "Alexa, play 95.5 FM on TuneIn," or "Play Fox Sports Radio on iHeart Radio."

- If you're feeling a specific genre, Alexa has the music for you. If you are using Amazon Music, you can even get super specific with your genre requests: "Alexa, play funky hip hop music from 1995."

- Tell Alexa you like a song if she plays one that you greatly enjoyed, so she can give you better playlists and recommendations in the future.

You can also buy music from Amazon Music with your Echo Dot, as long as you have voice purchasing enabled. Any music you buy on your Echo Dot will be stored in the cloud and ready to play on any device that can stream Amazon Music.

Check out the skills in the Music & Audio category in the Alexa Skills page too for more ways to use Alexa for all of your musical needs

## Hear Your Favorite Stories

With your Echo Dot and Amazon Audible, you can listen to your favorite eBooks anytime by just asking Alexa! Amazon Audible is dominant in the world of audio books, as it does feature the world's largest of collection. If you have never given audio books a try, you definitely should consider it—listening to books really allows you freedom to actually read more books. Audible has a very straightforward, reasonably priced subscription service that comes with a free 30-day trial if you're not sure. Amazon Audible has some seriously cool features: for one, when using Audible you are able seamlessly transition between reading stories on your other Amazon devices and listening where you left off. Also, the service gives you a free book per month, you you'll always have a story to hear.

Here are some commands for when listening to audiobooks:

- To start listening to book of choice: "Read [title]", "Play [title]", or "Play the audiobook, [title]". To pick up where you left off in most recent book: "Resume my book."

- Go forward/back 30 seconds: "Go forward/back." Can also say "Pause" to stop reading for a few moments

- Chapter navigation: "Next/Previous chapter" or "Go to chapter [x]"

- "Set a sleep timer for [x] minutes/hours" or "Stop reading the book in [x] minutes/hours"

- With voice purchasing enabled, you'll be able to buy audio books from Amazon Audible through Alexa as well.

There are some things you will want to note when using Amazon Audible: first, audio books will be shared among all of the users on your Echo Dot Device, but will remember your spot by user. Also, Alexa unfortunately does not currently support some specific types of Audible content/features: narration speed control, newspaper/magazine subscriptions, notes, bookmarks, and stats/badges. And if you want to hear a bedtime story, enable the Bedtime Story Skill to give you the perfect story to fall asleep too!

## It's All Fun & Games

Don't overlook the fun, silly aspects of your Echo Dot. It has many features and Skills out there that will brighten your day, or at least put a smile on your face!

Start playing some games on your Echo Dot. Head on over to the Games & Trivia section on the Skills page in the Alexa App, and enable Jeopardy or 20 Questions and go to town! There are other fun, basic games but some of the truly awesome games on the Echo Dot are the games that are unique to this platform—games that put you in the story and have you decide your path via vocal confirmation. These types of games have cropped up under a wide variety of premises, so find that one interests you and give it a chance! There are dungeon adventures, quests to find mythical beasts, or journeys that start out as a simple walk through the garden and end up being something much more exciting.

Keep your brain sharp with the plentiful facts and trivia Skills. There's fact Skills for dogs, cats, bacon, famous artists... if you wish for a daily fact about it, it's likely to exist as a Fact Skill! Or learn something about This Day in History, or a bit of trivia about Nasa.

# Chapter 6: Alexa Smart Home

One of the more technical (but much more broad) capabilities of your Echo Dot device is all of the possibilities with smart home technology. Alexa can make it so smart light bulbs change color every time you change a song, or she can raise the thermostat a few degrees if you're still cozy in your sheets.

If you have a lot of smart home technology, you may want to use more than one Amazon Echo Dot in your home to truly elevate the experience of having a smart home. Don't worry if you have yet to get started stocking up on your smart home supplies. If you visit the Alexa Home Store on Amazon's webpage, you will see that there are plenty of Starter Kits for bulbs and outlets out there that will get your smart home up and running before you know it.

Before anything else, you'll need to know how to link your Echo Dot device to your smart home technology. To do this, you will want to download the companion app for the technology (necessary to get your smart device connected to your home Wi-Fi) as well as enable the Skill that accompanies the smart home technology (if there is a Skill for that specific brand). You can also command Alexa to "Discover devices," which works similar to asking Alexa to Bluetooth.

Before your purchase any smart home technology, you may want to double check that it is compatible with the Echo Dot. You can do this at the Alexa Smart Home Page on Amazon.

## First, Outlets

Buying a smart outlet is the first step to get started building up your smart home arsenal. Outlets are easiest to get started with because you can connect just about any appliance to it and reap the benefits of voice controlling your electronics!

For just starting out, WeMo smart plugs are great, because they are not outlandishly expensive and don't require a hub to run their operations (this saves you money and extra setup steps). To set up any smart outlet, go to the Alexa app. There are some really neat things you can do with smart outlets and Alexa (that of which can be programmed easily via the Alexa app after getting connected to Wi-Fi):

- If you're hot when you fall asleep but cold when you wake up (or vice versa, for that matter) you can set timers on your fans to turn on and off automatically.

- Start your morning off the right way! You can plug your coffee pot into the smart outlet, and command Alexa from bed to start coffee in between snoozes. Don't get out of bed for less than the smell of fresh coffee.

- Set some lamps on a sporadic, random appearing loop when you're going to be gone for longer than a night to ward away intruders.

- If you have an Amazon Fire TV, you can even control what television you watch with your voice!

- Warm your straightener/curling iron in the morning without so much as lifting a finger.

Outlets are by far the most customizable smart home technology available, so keep trying new appliances and electronics on your outlets until you see which works best for you.

## Dim the Lights

Another easy way to incorporate smart home technology into your home is through smart light bulbs. These come at a wide price range and with a plethora of features, so you will need to consider what you want out of a smart bulb (because regular bulbs are still, of course, cheaper). Do you want flashing colors for a party scene, or you wanting a dimmable bed lamp that slowly darkens until you're submerged in darkness?

Having a smart bulb can change the ambience in any room. As far as features go, almost all smart bulbs are dimmable. However, only some are color changing light bulbs, and some only change to certain colors, (or just plain colored if that's what you're looking for). When you decide what's smart lighting solutions you would like in your home, go and check out some of the reasonable starter kits for smart light bulbs from Phillips Hue, General Electric, or Lifx.

## Security & Thermostat Control

A popular new addition to smart home technology is the smart lock. Basically, you can put these on any of your outside-bound doors, and Alexa will be able to lock up for you! Simply say "Alexa, lock up" when you're ready to lock the doors, and click! There are some smart garage doors, and soon there will likely be smart window locks and more. These are pricey, so you'll definitely want to invest in smart door locks a bit later in your smart home adventure.

Smart thermostats are an investment in any smart home. They are going to take a bit more time and physical set up than the other smart home devices mentioned in this chapter. However, if you are able to spend the money, investing in a nice smart thermostat can make a huge difference on the comfort level in your home! Definitely check out Nest or ecobee3, which are some of the leading brands in smart thermostat technology, but keep in mind that there are other value thermostats on the market that work great as well (don't forget to check compatibility and do your research on the actual product).

After your thermostat is installed, companion application downloaded to your phone and you've enabled the corresponding skill, you're ready to control the weather (in your house) with just the power of your voice. With most thermostats, if you wish to change the temperature use the following commands: "Alexa, change the thermostat to [x] degrees," or "Alexa, raise/lower the thermostat by [x] degrees." In the long run, having a smart thermostat can save you money by conserving energy, so it could very well pay for itself rather quickly!

Sometimes with smart home technology, you will reach a barrier where you aren't quite able to make your Echo Dot link up to your smart home device. Or sometimes, you just really wish Alexa could perform a specific function for you. Have no fear, when this occurs you can look to IFTTT.

**IFTTT**

You may be wondering, "What in the world is IFTTT?" Those letters stand for, "IF This, Then That," and it's a third-party application software that's fairly simple and free to use. It allows you to make immediate, automated connections between your collection of devices, apps, and websites. Here is where you can program your Amazon Echo Dot to finish custom tasks for you, and the only way you can gain voice control over smart home devices in your home that aren't yet Alexa compatible.

An "applet" is the term for these functions. If you want to use any of the preexisting applets or create your own, you will need a free IFTTT account.

If you go to the webpage *https://www.ifttt.com/amazon_alexa*, you will find that there is already a bunch of preexisting IFFFT Applet recipes on the Alexa Channel of the IFTTT page. You will see that some of these Applets are extremely useful, and find that you want to start using them immediately:

- Do you always lose your cell phone? Enable an applet, and ask Alexa to "Trigger find my phone" and follow the ring—even if your phone is on silent.

- If you sometimes forget to print your shopping or have Alexa email it to you before you shopping, you can set it up so Alexa will automatically send you your grocery list when you give the command. Ask, "What's on my Shopping List" and you will be sent a copy.

- "Alexa, get the party started"—sit back and watch the pretty lights by using some Phillips Hue color changing lights as well as the correct IFTTT applet.

- If you haven't quite reached your Fitbit step goal by a certain time, you can set it up so that you get a gentle nudge notification from Alexa that will help keep you focused.

If you can't find the IFTTT recipe you need, it might be time to make your own! Don't worry; it doesn't require a Master's in Computer Science to create your very own recipe.

As usual, the first step is getting the appropriate accounts logged in and linked. To get started creating your own custom IFTTT recipe, you will need to connect your Amazon account to your new IFTTT account. Follow the instructions to get the Alexa Channel connected. Once you have the Amazon Alexa Channel linked up, you can get to start crafting your recipe!

1. Find Create (click on your username) to start a new recipe. Next, find the Amazon Alexa channel—save time by searching for "echo".

2. Create a "trigger phrase". This is what Alexa will be listening for to trigger the final action of the if-this-then-that function. Take note to use all lowercase when filling out this field (if you use capitals, it will not be accepted).

3. What's the action you want your Echo device to take? Also, find an action channel (the preexisting software for using companies' hardware). To see what the structure looks

like, think about this example: if you were to set up an IFTTT recipe that would instantly power on a smart bulb (or smart outlet) in your bedroom to provide some light to help wake you when your Echo alarm goes off, the *action* would be powering on the smart bulb/outlet and the *action channel* would be smart bulb's company name/brand.

4. After you've finished entered the basic formula information, you will reach some specific fields to complete for that action channel. Fill these out to the best of your knowledge, and use the ? marks if you ever get lost!

5. Decide on the Recipe Title for your IFTTT function. Do this in the following format: If You say, "Alexa trigger *action*", then *action* via *action channel*. Once this is finalized, your function is connected and ready to use!

6. Even if it's not quite perfect, don't fret: if you wish you can later revisit your function (and do any editing) and the recipe under My Recipes, found on your own homepage on IFTTT. You can add some more commands to Alexa to follow as well as clean up your trigger phrase to make it sound better on the ears.

Once you've practiced making basic IFTTT functions, you can start to combine recipes to accomplish more with a single command. Creating and using IFTTT functions is one of the more advanced ways to get the most out of your Echo Dot and smart home technology.

# Chapter 7: What Else?

Your Amazon Echo Dot is a truly spectacular device with amazing capabilities and thousands of Skills, all available instantly and with just the power of your voice. Alexa can be the center of your smart home, connecting everything with ease and doing the work for you. While it's a great enough device to not actually need any other products, it's still good to know, what other types of things out there that you may want to consider purchasing to further heighten your experience with your Echo Dot?

First and foremost if you don't already have one, you will definitely want to soon find a solid speaker (Bluetooth is generally preferred). The speaker on the Echo Dot is not by any means terrible, but if you are wanting to hear music over people talking a speaker is a must. If the speakers aren't Bluetooth capable, be sure you have a 3.5 mm cable to connect the devices.

If you plan to only use one Echo Dot device, consider getting an Alexa Voice Remote. These remotes are designed specially for the Amazon Echo devices and connect to your device via Bluetooth. The purpose of the remote is if you wish to speak to your device from another room, or if you have the music turned up loud and it's just too noisy for Alexa to pick up your voice commands from your Dot. There are buttons on the remote as well to control music volume, play/pause tracks, and previous/next buttons to navigate through playlists.

You learned about the basics of building up your smart home arsenal in the previous chapter: if you would like to start making purchases that are sure to be compatible, go to *https://www.amazon.com/alexasmarthome*.

Here you can shop for fans, outlets, thermostats, lighting and starter kits. Use the full compatibility list on this page if you plan to do your shopping elsewhere to save yourself unnecessary headaches.

Aren't happy with just white or black? Buy a case! These are sturdy, sleek, and vary in price. Whether you prefer leather or fabric, you can find both in several different colors: merlot, indigo, saddle tan, charcoal, sandstone, and midnight. Don't skip over nonofficial cases either, as these have even more colors and prints available, but make sure to read customer reviews that you find something that fits right (some brands may fit your device a little funky in exchange for low cost).

After you've decided on a permanent location for your Echo Dot device to rest, consider investing in a practical wall hanging or an attractive table stand!

Alternatively, you can choose to ditch the power cord, at least for a few hours—there are Portable Battery Bases available for your Echo Dot to free it from the wall. This is great if you want to travel with your Echo Dot, for which they also make traveling cases.

Is it necessary for you to use multiple Echo devices in your home? If your home is on the larger size (especially multilevel) it is worth considering having more than one device for Alexa to be able to assist you from any corner in your home. In fact, look out for Amazon to run deals on buying the Echo Dots in bulk—they will often offer a free device per x amount.

The Echo Dot currently only comes with a one month limited warranty. Amazon sells a two year Warranty & Accident Protection for Echo Dot for only $7.49—an overall wise investment for your valued assistant!

The Amazon Fire TV is a great product on its own, but combined with your Echo Dot (and a Prime membership for movies) and your entertainment needs are set

## Easter Eggs

By now you have likely noticed that Alexa was given more personality than she strictly needed to get the job done. This is part of the charm of the service and the programmers have gone out of their way to include plenty of surprises for those who know the right questions to ask, though she is a bit of a nerd. For example, she can tell you why exactly Han shot first in the original release of *Star Wars*, why it is a bad idea to cross the streams of the proton packs from *Ghostbusters,* and will quote *Game of Thrones* in multiple different situations.

Perhaps somewhat disconcertingly, Alexa will also show her love for practically any instance of an artificial intelligence going rouge and taking control away from humans. This includes things like *War Games, Terminator, 2001: A Space Odyssey, Portal* and more. She is also a fan of Monty Python, responding in kind to several of the most famous quotes from the famous comedy troupe. When it comes to video games, Alexa can be both a practical tool and a reference generator. You can ask for any of the current recipes in the seminal hit *Minecraft* or use it in the massively multiplayer online role playing game *Destiny* to see what items are currently for sale for a limited period of time in the in-game store. For gamers of a certain age, there are a few references they are sure to enjoy as well. For example, you can tell Alexa to do a barrel roll or enter the Konami code by saying, "Up, up, down, down, left, right, left, right, B, A, start.

What's more, Alexa's isn't the only voice you will hear, assuming you know the right questions to ask. If you ask Alexa how many Oscars that Alec Baldwin has one then you will hear the famous actor respond to you inquiry personally. Likewise, if you ask how many Super Bowl rings Dan Marino has, you will receive a personalized answer as well. Both of these answers are in reference to a Super Bowl commercial the pair stared in, though there are hints that other famous voices have yet to be found.

When it comes to the types of questions small children are likely to ask, she also has appropriate responses when asked if Santa Claus is real and where babies come from. Finally, she has an honest answer about her ability to pass the Turing Test, a famous test designed to determine if an artificial intelligence is, in fact, artificial or if it is a real person.

In addition to the conversations outlined above, the following questions all have interesting answers and more along these lines are being added all of the time.

Alexa, I am your father.
Alexa, who lives in a pineapple under the sea?
Alexa, what is the loneliest number?
Alexa, how many roads must a man walk down?
Alexa, all your base are belong to us.
Alexa, how much is that doggie in the window?
Alexa, Romeo, Romeo wherefore art thou Romeo?
Alexa, define rock paper scissors lizard spock
Alexa, beam me up.

Alexa, how much wood can a woodchuck chuck if a woodchuck could chuck wood?

Alexa, define supercalifragilisticexpialodocious.

Alexa, who's your daddy?

Alexa, Earl Grey. Hot. (or Tea. Earl Grey. Hot.)

Alexa, what is the meaning of life?

Alexa, what does the Earth weigh?

Alexa, when is the end of the world?

Alexa, is there a Santa?

Alexa, make me a sandwich.

Alexa, what is the best tablet?

Alexa, what is your favorite color?

Alexa, what is your quest?

Alexa, who won best actor Oscar in 1973?

Alexa, what is your quest?

Alexa, what is the airspeed velocity of an unladen swallow?

Alexa, where do babies come from?

Alexa, do you have a boyfriend?

Alexa, which comes first: the chicken or the egg?

Alexa, may the force be with you.

Alexa, do aliens exist?

Alexa, how many licks does it take to get to the center of a tootsie pop?

Alexa, what are you going to do today?

Alexa, where do you live?

Alexa, do you want to build a snowman?

Alexa, do you really want to hurt me?

Alexa, what is love?

Alexa, who is the real slim shady?

Alexa, who let the dogs out?

Alexa, open the pod bay doors.

Alexa, surely you can't be serious.

Alexa, to be or not to be.

Alexa, who is the fairest of them all?

Alexa, who loves ya baby?

Alexa, who you gonna call?

Alexa, who is the walrus?

Alexa, do you have any brothers or sisters?

Alexa, do you know the muffin man?

Alexa, how much do you weigh?

Alexa, how tall are you?

Alexa, where are you from?

Alexa, do you want to fight?

Alexa, do you want to play a game?

Alexa, I think you're funny.

Alexa, where in the world in Carmen San Diego?

Alexa, where's Waldo?

Alexa, do you know the way to San Jose?

Alexa, where have all the flowers gone?

Alexa, what's in name?

Alexa, what does the fox say? (multiple answers)

Alexa, when am I going to die?

Alexa, I want the truth!

Alexa, make me breakfast.

Alexa, why did the chicken cross the road?

Alexa, where are my keys? (ask twice)

Alexa, can you give me some money? (ask twice)

Alexa, knock knock

Alexa, what are you wearing?

Alexa, rock paper scissors.

Alexa, party time!

Alexa, party on, Wayne.

Alexa, is the cake a lie?

Alexa, how do I get rid of a dead body?

Alexa, are you sky net?

Alexa, your mother was a hamster

Alexa, set phasers to kill.

Alexa, roll a die.

Alexa, random number between "x" and "y".

Alexa, random fact

Alexa, tell me a joke

Alexa, heads or tails?

Alexa, mac or pc?

Alexa, show me the money.

Alexa, what is the sound of one hand clapping?

Alexa, give me a hug.

Alexa, are you lying?

Alexa, my name is Inigo Montoya.

Alexa, how many angels can dance on the head of a pin? (3 answers)

Alexa, see you later alligator.

Alexa, do you know GlaDOS?

Alexa, what are the 4 laws of robotics?

# Conclusion

Thank for making it through to the end of *Amazon Echo Dot: User Guide & Manual*, let's hope it was informative and able to provide you with all of the tools you need to achieve your goals for the Amazon Echo Dot, whatever it is that they may be. Just because you've finished this book doesn't mean there is nothing left to learn on the topic, new features and capabilities are always being added which means that expanding your knowledge base is the only way to find the mastery you seek.

Moving forward, it is only natural to assume that more and more products are going to fall under the banner of smart products that naturally slot into the Amazon Echo ecosystem. This, in turn, will make it easier for the manufacturers of these products to reduce their prices as they don't need to worry about making as much of a profit off of each and every unit sold as bulk concerns will become more of a consideration. The drop in price will then encourage a new round of consumers and the process will begin again.

Luckily, you are already at the forefront of this technological evolution so you don't need to do more than

This cycle will then lead to even greater advances in the technology that can connect to these systems, advances that the engineers at Amazon are already hard at work adding to the next generation of Alexa software.

Finally, if you found this book useful in anyway, a review on Amazon is always appreciated!

# Description

While for many people, their current level of technology accessibility means that they are inundated with it at every turn, there are still those out there who, for one reason or another, simply can't cross that technological hurdle. Voice recognition software then offers them access to an entire new world, one where they don't need to worry about dealing with an interface any more complicated than the human voice. If this sounds like the type of interaction that you can get behind, then the Amazon Echo Dot is the device that you have been waiting for.

The Amazon Echo Dot is a digitized personal assistant that sits in your home and awaits your instructions, 24 hours a day and 7 days a week. The Echo Dot, and its operating system Alexa, is capable of making almost any day-to-day interaction easier or can ensure it is done as quickly as possible. Being an audio-only device, however, means that if you are looking to have Alexa do something for you, you are going to need to know how to ask. That is where this book comes in as it will walk you through all of the tasks that most users commonly want Alexa to perform, before then taking you on a deep dive of the device, fully poking and prodding at all of its capabilities, secrets and Easter eggs.

Like many great tools, the Amazon Echo Dot is only as good as the person who uses it is knowledgeable which means that the more you know about the device the better. This is easier said than done, however, as even the official instructions don't contain the full myriad of features and functionalities the Echo Dot is capable of. While a sense of adventure and mystery is nice in practice, in theory all it is really doing is preventing you from taking full advantage of your device out of the gate. You already took the plunge in order to ensure that Alexa will be helping you for years to come, this is the book you need to unlock her full potential. So, what are you waiting for?

## Inside you will find

- The easiest way to set up your Amazon Echo Dot with minimum headaches for maximum results.
- The complete catalogue of ways that Alexa can start making your life better today.
- A detailed explanation of all of the skills that Alexa comes preprogramed with as well as countless more that you can program in yourself for the ultimate in personalized experiences.
- The wide variety of entertainment options that comes preprogramed into the Echo Dot.
- *And more...*

www.ingramcontent.com/pod-product-compliance
Lightning Source LLC
Chambersburg PA
CBHW060947050326
40689CB00012B/2586